AF599185

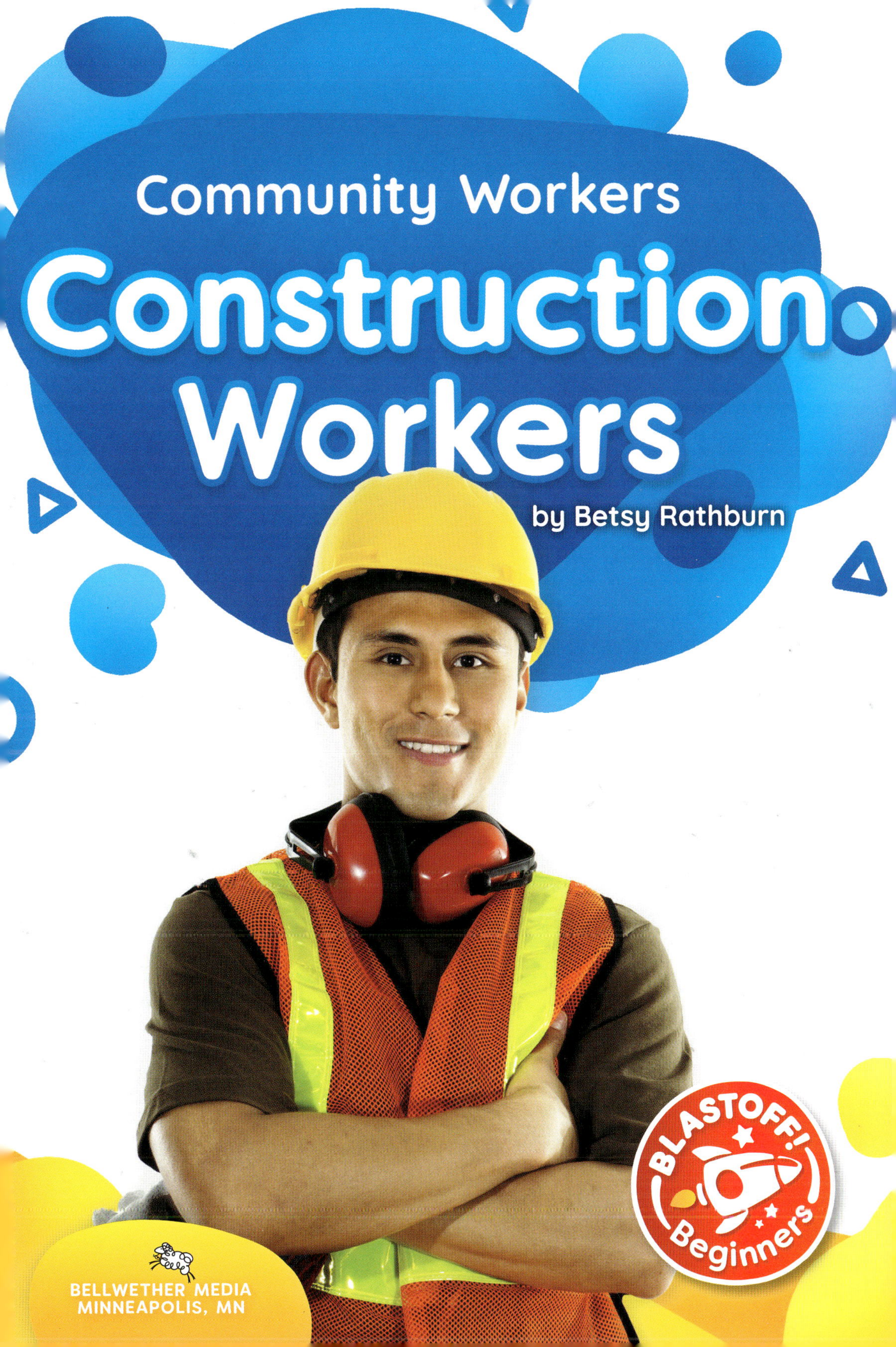
Community Workers
Construction Workers
by Betsy Rathburn
BLASTOFF! Beginners
BELLWETHER MEDIA
MINNEAPOLIS, MN

Blastoff! Beginners are developed by literacy experts and educators to meet the needs of early readers. These engaging informational texts support young children as they begin reading about their world. Through simple language and high frequency words paired with crisp, colorful photos, Blastoff! Beginners launch young readers into the universe of independent reading.

Sight Words in This Book

and
at
big
help
look
on
saw
the
them
these
they
too
use
we

This edition first published in 2025 by Bellwether Media, Inc.

No part of this publication may be reproduced in whole or in part without written permission of the publisher. For information regarding permission, write to Bellwether Media, Inc., Attention: Permissions Department, 6012 Blue Circle Drive, Minnetonka, MN 55343.

Library of Congress Cataloging-in-Publication Data

LC record for Construction Workers available at: https://lccn.loc.gov/2024004936

Text copyright © 2025 by Bellwether Media, Inc. BLASTOFF! BEGINNERS and associated logos are trademarks and/or registered trademarks of Bellwether Media, Inc. Bellwether Media is a division of Chrysalis Education Group.

Editor: Rebecca Sabelko Designer: Laura Sowers

Printed in the United States of America, North Mankato, MN.

Table of Contents

On the Job

Look at the construction workers! They wear **hard hats**.

hard hats

What Are They?

Construction workers build things. They work on **job sites**.

job site

They build houses and offices.

They build roads and bridges.

BOW MARK
FINNING
GRADE CONTROL
Asphalt and Concrete Construction

What Do They Do?

These workers look at **blueprints**. The plans help them work.

blueprints

They use tools.
They use
hammers
and saws.

saw

hammer

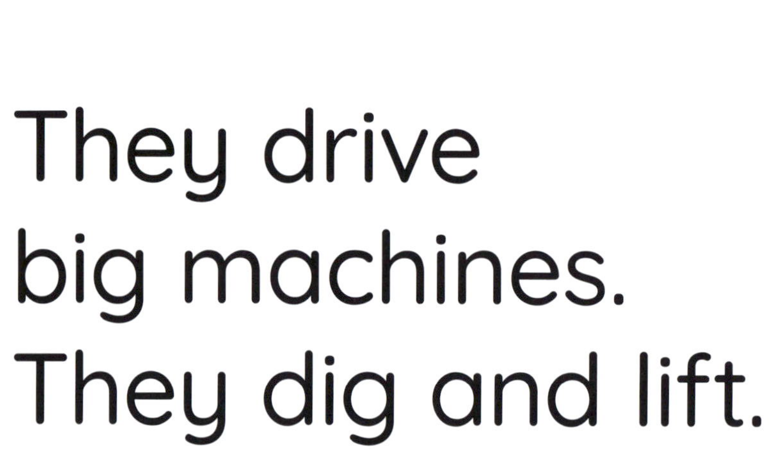

They drive
big machines.
They dig and lift.

They stay safe. They wear bright colors. Hard hats help, too!

Why Do We Need Them?

These workers work hard. They build things we need!

Construction Worker Facts

Tools

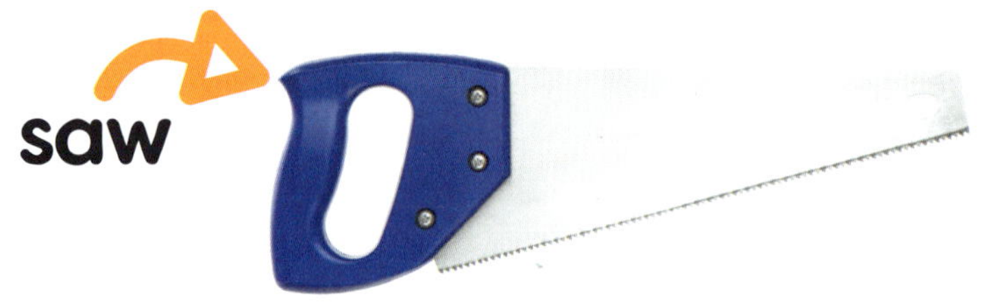

A Day in the Life

look at blueprints

use tools

drive big machines

Glossary

blueprints

plans that show how something will be made

hammers

tools that construction workers use to hit things

hard hats

hats that help keep construction workers safe

job sites

places where construction workers work

To Learn More

ON THE WEB

FACTSURFER

Factsurfer.com gives you a safe, fun way to find more information.

1. Go to www.factsurfer.com.
2. Enter "construction workers" into the search box and click 🔍.
3. Select your book cover to see a list of related content.

Index

The images in this book are reproduced through the courtesy of: iodrakon, front cover; Serhiy Kobyakov, p. 3; Lertsakwiman, p. 4; Monkey Business Images, pp. 4-5; Roman023_photography, pp. 6-7; jhorrocks, pp. 8-9; constantgardener, pp. 10-11; GEORGII MIRONOV, p. 12 (blueprints); PeopleImages, pp. 12-13; Veniamin Kraskov, p. 14 (saw); Kehinde Olufemi Akinbo, pp. 14-15; Boarding1Now, pp. 16-17; Lisa F. Young, p. 18; The Art of Pics, pp. 18-19; sturti, pp. 20-21; Tatiana Popova, p. 22 (saw); WiP-Studio, p. 22 (hard hat); Far700, p. 22 (hammer); Ground Picture, p. 22 (look at blueprints); Authentic Images, p. 22 (use tools); Phynart Studio, p. 22 (drive big machines); Gargantiopa, p. 23 (blueprints); NassornSnitwong, p. 23 (hammers); Blue Titan, p. 23 (hard hats); Iryna Liveoak, p. 23 (job sites).